D0843303

Ruth M. Shelly
PO Box 115
Oley, PA 19547

GROWING UP PLAIN

Witty and confessional memories
from the adolescence of a "plain" Mennonite girl

SHIRLEY KURTZ

Intercourse, PA 17534
Printed in Mexico

Design by Dawn J. Ranck

GROWING UP PLAIN

Intercourse, Pennsylvania 17534
International Standard Book Number: 1-56148-103-3
Library of Congress Catalog Card Number: 94-17300

Printed in Mexico.

Library of Congress Cataloging-in-Publication Data

Kurtz, Shirley.
Growing up plain : witty and confessional memories from the adolescence of a "plain" Mennonite girl / Shirley Kurtz.
p. cm.
ISBN 1-56148-103-3 : $9.95
1. Kurtz, Shirley. 2. Women, Mennonite—Pennsylvania—Biography.
3. Children of clergy—Pennsylvania—Biography. I. Title.
BX8143.K87A3 1994
289.7'092—dc20
[B] 94-17300
CIP

My mother says we were over at the Leamans when this picture was taken. Isn't she beautiful! Just look at her sitting there with me in her lap and my brother on the ottoman and my father holding our dolly. Later there would be four more children. I am amazed at the glow on the faces in these early pictures, when my parents were untroubled and young and hopeful and we could be held and carried around and tucked in at night and didn't talk back.

Contents

1.
Envying Gloria

There was some trouble with being plain.

When my mother first put up my long hair in a bun, to go under a covering, I imagined that now I would look like Betty Keener, an older girl I admired who came to the mission sometimes to help out.

(I was about eleven.)

I went outside and walked up and down the sidewalk a little, feeling important. But when I looked in the mirror my hair wasn't like Betty's. No amount of dreaming was going to make me somebody else.

I wasn't going to look like Gloria, either.

My best friend Gloria and I got baptized together, the same day, at the mission where my father was the preacher. So now we wore coverings. But she was allowed to wear her hair *sticking out.*

Aunt Naomi is the one in the middle with short hair and stylish clothes and probably makeup. She'd left the Mennonite church years ago and hardly ever came to reunions.

My mother said hair was supposed to be long and pretty much covered up. Some of my aunts (we saw the aunts about once a year, at reunions) probably thought my covering wasn't big enough. Aunt Mary Louise's came the whole way front to her hairline, practically. I didn't feel so plain at reunions.

Certainly nobody back home in Steelton could have thought I was too worldly.

We lived at the Mennonite mission on the West Side in Steelton, Pennsylvania. Part of the big old building had once been a store, but now it was made into a chapel, with benches and a pulpit. The storefront windows were still there, and the creaky wood floors. Along the wall on the women's side (men and women didn't sit together in church) was a door that opened right into our kitchen.

I was embarrassed about the linoleum in our living room. It was good for mop rides, at least. We did

On the corner of Myers and Conestoga, Steelton.

eventually get new linoleum, but is new linoleum much better than old linoleum in your *living room*?

The mission had apartments and an attic and a big cellar (good for roller skating) and lots of bathrooms. But only one with a tub. We had to share it with Mr. and Mrs. Shrauder (elderly town people, not Mennonites) in the second floor apartment, and the mission sisters who lived up on the third floor. Once Mrs. Shrauder got so disgusted because somebody had used her towel (probably by mistake).

Another Steelton person, old Mary Hollenbaugh, didn't live with us, but she'd come Sunday afternoons—just turn the doorknob and push open the door and walk in. She'd sit in our rocking chair for a long while and not say much. Click her false teeth and grumble a little, maybe say she was constipated. Once my brother hid the big tape recorder behind the rocking chair, ahead of time, and after she left we tried

1960. My father must be the one pulling the mop.

1963

to listen to the recording. But it was mostly just the squeaks from the rocking chair.

We played a trick on Skeechball too, one time; Skeechball was the town kid who bullied everybody. My brother tied long thin pieces of wire (the wire was so thin you could hardly see it) onto the arms of our floppy clown doll. Then he took it upstairs to my father's study with the long front windows that stuck out high over the sidewalk, and he lowered the doll over a windowsill and down onto the pavement. When we saw Skeechball coming, my brother pulled on the wires to make the doll dance. Didn't Skeechball's eyes just about bulge! We thought we even scared him some.

Across the street from us was a beer joint and a big outdoor skating rink; also the firehouse. One year Betty Klinger down the street was queen of the firemen's convention. (My brother was friends with her brother Chester who had an actual pet monkey.) She rode atop the back of a car in the firemen's parade. Our house was near the end of the parade route, and going past us she could hardly wave or smile anymore, she was so tired. But her gown was gorgeous. She was gorgeous.

(How I loved the finery! Whenever I heard the honking horns that meant a wedding I would race to the window. The car with the tin cans and streamers would be flying past, and I'd catch a glimpse of the bride scrunched up against the groom in the back seat and floating in all her incredible dreamy finery.)

All day long, in the summers, old men loafed on the benches outside the firehouse. My mother didn't see how men could just sit around all day; they had to be doing something questionable. She told my brothers to stay away.

Sometimes there were carnivals at the skating rink.

Betty Klinger on the way to the convention to get crowned.

We were allowed to go over and buy a hot dog, but we had to come home to eat it. We'd sit behind the darkened church windows and watch the Ferris wheel and bingo games. We wondered why bingo was wrong if the money went for the firehouse or a church, and my parents said bingo was unnecessary. You could just put the money in the offering.

Of course we stayed out of the beer joint. It was dark in there and mysterious. We children would sit on our front steps and smell the odors. We didn't know what beer smelled like; we smelled the French fries.

I don't think there were a whole lot of people wanting to join our church and become Mennonites. We didn't get much acquainted with the old couple who lived next door, but once when Mrs. Wrightstone was on her porch some of us children sang to her from inside our house, "Ye Must Be Born Again."

And I went out and rounded up the little

neighborhood children, sometimes, and brought them to our yard for a Bible story. Afterwards I'd feed them something. Once I was stirring up a big jar of Kool-Aid, for the children. I was stirring hard and the spoon was banging against the sides of the jar, and then of course the glass cracked and there was Kool-Aid puddled on the kitchen table and running down the oilcloth onto the floor. I guess I learned my lesson about stirring things in jars.

Some days instead of rounding up little kids I was out peddling things. I helped the other church people pass out tracts. We'd stick the papers on everybody's porches—under doormats or in milk boxes so they wouldn't blow away.

I peddled taffy, too, but this was entirely a business venture. Summer afternoons my mother would let me boil the taffy and pour it while it was still hot and runny into muffin pans, to harden, and then wrap each little round piece in wax paper. It was vinegar candy in the cookbook, but we called it taffy so people would buy it.

My sister and I would tramp around town with the taffy; also Rice Krispies candy. I thought Rice Krispies candy was kind of disgusting and tough, after it was a few hours old, and if customers said they didn't want any today because they still had some left from last week, I thought they might be lying.

People had to come to our house for the popsicles. We made them out of Kool-Aid. My father would bring home long skinny pieces of wood and cut them up with the jigsaw, for the popsicle sticks. Some kid would be at the door with his money, and we'd go running to the freezer at the opposite end of the house and come running back with whatever flavor the kid wanted. My mother would wipe up the hall.

And kids would come just to play. Georgie Getz and

Barbie Feldman with my sister.

Dennis Crumlich and Eladio Maroquin. Barbie Feldman and Tonya Husick and Judy Maldonovich and Irene Easter. Barbie Feldman had cancans. Stick-out slips, we called them. Rita Zerbe (she was older, not a playmate) would walk by in her short shorts. She was incredible. None of these town girls were Mennonite; my sister and I couldn't ever expect to be like *them*.

But Gloria! I was justifiably envious. She lived in a white farmhouse in the country. (Her parents drove up to Steelton on Sundays and Wednesday nights and helped with Club and Bible School.) She had four sisters—three of them older, and I guess I worshiped them. All the girls were pretty. They could wear skirts and blouses (not always cape dresses, like I had to wear), and white shoes in the summertime, and the older ones had boyfriends. I loved going to Gloria's.

I suppose she had fun at my house, too. Once we

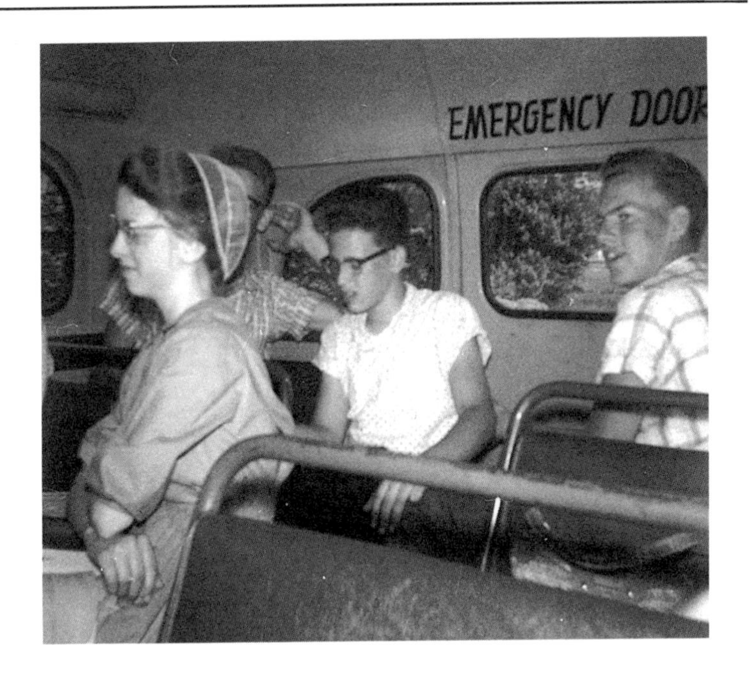

Another seeming injustice: Mennonite boys could look pretty ordinary.

were playing doctor with our little sisters, and we tried to feed her sister Vicks—or was it Vaseline?—covered up with some Cheerios, in a spoon.

Gloria was a wonderful friend. She never said I was plain and deprived. And she stuck by me on the bus and at school.

My father drove the bus. Don't ask me how he managed to be a preacher *and* a school bus driver *and* the principal at the Mennonite school.

2.
Sores Behind My Ears

The bus ride was very long—my feet would about go numb from the cold on winter mornings. The bus would chug out of Steelton and lurch round the windy country roads picking up the Mennonites here and there. We had to ride for a whole hour—the school was near Mount Joy, Pennsylvania.

We all had our lunchboxes along. The best lunch, I thought, was bean soup in my thermos and a chicken salad sandwich. (My mother would grind up some cold chicken and add pickles and Miracle Whip, for the chicken salad.)

I'd started school when I was five. When Mrs. Murphy would let us little ones out for recess, we'd play house under the biggest oldest tree in the schoolyard. It had an enormous fat trunk and we'd make rooms in the dirt, with stones lined up for the walls. Later on, maybe in the fifth grade, in Miss Hess's room, we'd make our houses on the blackboard, instead. You could look inside and see the upstairs and downstairs and all the furniture.

(Much later, when I was an adult writing my first children's book, *The Boy and the Quilt,* I asked the artist to put in a house like that. Of course the house in the book was much lovelier than anything we could ever draw in the fifth grade with regular old white chalk.)

I won't tell you the name of my seventh grade teacher. She had thirteen dresses, if we counted right. We were terrible that year. In the seventh grade it is almost impossible to behave if your teacher doesn't make you behave, so I think the bedlam was really her fault. (Certainly it is not her fault, anymore, when I don't behave.) My mother seems to think seventh grade is when I lost my scholarly diligence.

I have a memory of naughty Gerald Ruhl not in his seat but up on a sort of shelf above the closet. Had he clambered up there on his own? Or did the teacher have him there for a punishment? If so, he was working the situation to his advantage. Who could study with Gerald Ruhl monkeying around up there on the shelf?

It was in seventh grade, or maybe eighth, when Gloria and I and one or two other girls tried to do the goat song in front of the class. Probably it was during a Friday afternoon program; certainly we'd practiced. In the song the goat ate three red shirts off the washline and for his mischief got tied to the railroad tracks:

And when the train came into sight,
That goat grew pale and green with fright;
He heaved a sigh, as if in pain,
Coughed up those shirts and flagged the train—

at which point we were going to whip out the big red hankies we were hiding behind our backs and wave them at the audience. But we couldn't get to the end of our song; we'd gone into a fit of giggling. Have you ever in a grave situation (we were *up front*) collapsed like this? If one girl got hold of herself, momentarily, another one fell apart. We were watery-eyed, red, out of breath, embarrassed, and absolutely helpless.

Just looking at the picture (next page), you probably can't imagine any of us going into hysterics. There's Gloria in the middle of the top row. I'm in the same row, over on the right, between Elvin Kraybill and Nelson Keener. It looks like Elvin and I are practically touching.

For a while I had a picture of Elvin on my bedroom wall, in a frame made out of popsicle sticks. And he gave me a pair of soft black gloves with little red flowers embroidered on them, for my twelfth birthday,

Seventh and eighth graders with Miss Miller (not the one with 13 dresses).

but it was at a party my mother was having for me, and everybody else was giving me presents, too. So how could I know, just from the gloves, if Elvin actually liked me?

(My mother made beautiful snowball cupcakes—the snow was coconut—and my class from school came the whole way up to Steelton, and we all sat around in the living room and didn't know what to say.)

If you *were* boyfriend and girlfriend at our school, you didn't touch, except maybe hold hands. Nobody *kissed.* Once, though, Linda Stoner and I practiced kissing (on each other) so we would be prepared for in the future.

Nelson Keener said he liked me. People who were boyfriend and girlfriend always stood outside together after school, so I went outside after school and stood with Nelson. But then my father said I must stop doing this and I was relieved, because I wasn't sure I was in

Elvin

Nelson

love. I wasn't lovesick like I got sometimes. Maybe Nelson was relieved, too.

I should tell you about Ginnie Mummau. She's the one in the dark blouse in the middle row, in the picture. She was so jolly and funny and lively, and a good friend—I got to go to her house overnight. (There were windowsills big enough to sit in, and two pianos, if I'm remembering right. She and her sister would play wonderful loud thumping music.)

When Jeanne Wert (sitting on the grass, second from the left) started coming to our school I hoped she'd be my friend, too, but some other girls got her instead. Jeanne Wert wore cinch belts. (My mother said cinch belts made you look like a wasp.) And she wore bobby socks over her nylons. (Girls were required to wear long stockings.)

Jeanne and Ginnie and Gloria and who-all else could wear skirts and blouses to school, but not me. I was

We wore stoles in winter, or scarves. The trouble with stoles was they'd squash and wrinkle your covering.

stuck with capes. A cape was supposed to hide your shape, if you had any. There was this extra piece of material that matched your dress and fit over your shoulders and came down to your waist in front and back. (If you can't figure this out, look again at that picture of the boys in the back of the school bus, and me with my cape sort of flapping out behind.)

Here I was going to school with other Mennonites, which should have been some comfort. Well, it *was* a comfort. I would have gotten stared at, for sure, if I'd gone to the public school in Steelton. But at the Mennonite school I had to deal with the fact that I was plainER. Maybe plainER was worse than just *different.*

Capes were in the Mennonite rules, but as you can see, some parents weren't making their girls wear them. I fussed loudly at my mother about capes, but neither she nor my father had made the rules, and they were in no position to advocate rebellion. What could

That's John Murphy in the back. Probably the teacher should have had him in the front row.

my mother do? How could she make me happy?

In my spare time I drew up an imaginary wardrobe, tediously listing all the outfits. I thought up wedding color schemes (for in the future). My sister and I would go through the Sears catalog picking out the prettiest woman on each page. And I wrote stories. Rene was me; she was fourteen by now and her trouble was real.

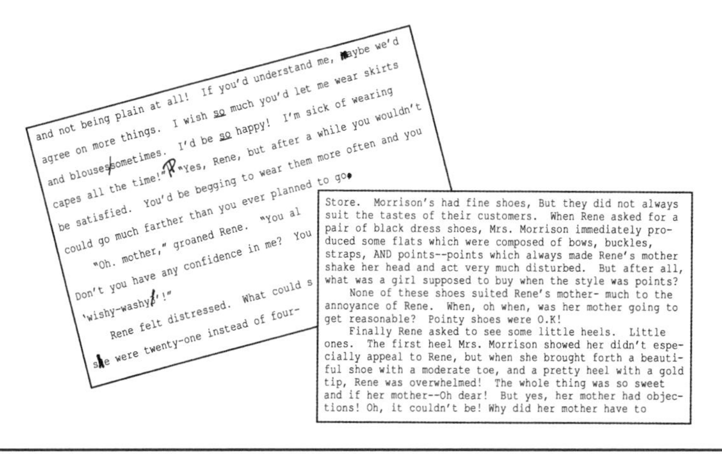

and not being plain at all! If you'd understand me, maybe we'd agree on more things. I wish so much you'd let me wear skirts and blouses sometimes. I'd be so happy! I'm sick of wearing capes all the time!" "Yes, Rene, but after a while you wouldn't be satisfied. You'd be begging to wear them more often and you could go much farther than you ever planned to go.

"Oh. mother," groaned Rene. "You al

Don't you have any confidence in me? You

'wishy-washy'!"

Rene felt distressed. What could s

she were twenty-one instead of four-

Store. Morrison's had fine shoes, But they did not always suit the tastes of their customers. When Rene asked for a pair of black dress shoes, Mrs. Morrison immediately produced some flats which were composed of bows, buckles, straps, AND points--points which always made Rene's mother shake her head and act very much disturbed. But after all, what was a girl supposed to buy when the style was points?

None of these shoes suited Rene's mother- much to the annoyance of Rene. When, oh when, was her mother going to get reasonable? Pointy shoes were O.K!

Finally Rene asked to see some little heels. Little ones. The first heel Mrs. Morrison showed her didn't especially appeal to Rene, but when she brought forth a beautiful shoe with a moderate toe, and a pretty heel with a gold tip, Rene was overwhelmed! The whole thing was so sweet and if her mother--Oh dear! But yes, her mother had objections! Oh, it couldn't be! Why did her mother have to

You have to understand this: my mother was doing her best. (And she didn't have just me to contend with. There was my sister, too. And my brothers could be every bit as nasty as yours; they called me *Fat Lips,* and *Hairy Kneecaps.*) My mother *wanted* me to be happy. We'd pick out the prettiest materials we could find, and she sewed dress after dress for me. And she didn't scold me about my waves.

I must have had at least as many waves in my hair as Jeanne Wert and the others. In the nighttime I'd set my waves with bobby pins and then put a hair net over top, to control the frizz. Also, for a while we all thought it was stylish to wear our hair pulled tight back over our ears. I got sores behind my ears, from them being jammed against my glasses.

Unfortunately, vanity couldn't be too thwarted by rules and regulations. Being plain couldn't make you not proud. That was the real problem, I guess.

3.
Still Enough Hair for a Bun

It was in the dormitory one night at the Mennonite high school near Lancaster, Pennsylvania, where I chopped off some of my hair. There was still quite enough for a bun, but my mother would be sad.

We'd moved to the country, to a green house with two whole bathrooms all to ourselves and a pine floor in the living room. Now we were far from the loafers and beer joints and bingo games; also far enough from the high school for me to live in the dorm and come home just on weekends.

It was necessary to be absolutely stealthy in the dorm, for the matron prowled the halls. During study hours we could go to other girls' rooms only with permission. And of course after lights out (10 o'clock, maybe) we were all supposed to be in our beds. Just two girls in every room. I seem to remember the matron finding somebody in a closet once, in my room; I sort of think I was the one in the closet. If this was the case I must have hoped, when I heard the matron coming and dived into the closet, that she'd not notice our visitor wasn't me, in the dark. If this is what I thought, it didn't work. The matron had eyes like a cat.

The Mennonite rules about capes and coverings were strictly enforced at the school. The popular kids fumed about this all the time. But I wasn't complaining. Because now, with everybody in the same boat (at school, at least), I didn't have to be plainER.

It was the style now to puff the hair over our ears (we teased it), and when we were seniors we gave up on waves. We put great big rollers in at night to straighten our hair. Poor us, when the yearbook came out with all our pictures taken months ago while we

In the yearbook, left to right: Ruthie Angstadt, me, and Norma Barge. It wasn't just the matron with cat eyes.

were still in our bobbypins and hairnets phase. Now we looked funny even to ourselves.

Is that a cape I'm wearing in my senior picture? Well, yes. A cape could be at least interesting. Small tucks (darts) could be sewed in the front part, and then a girl had some shape, after all. And a cape could be cut low, like a jumper, or collared like a suit. Later somebody even invented the armhole cape, which was practically a vest. (We had good imaginations.)

One of the best dresses my mother ever made for me for school had pleats all around, stitched partway down and ironed sharp the rest of the way. I was especially proud, going to classes, the days I wore that dress. It was brown plaid.

We scurried from dorm to classrooms and library and auditorium; our teachers we tolerated or possibly admired. One had awful fish breath (rotten *dead* fish). My geometry teacher, Mrs. Eby, was cool—so articulate and precise and calculated, so absolutely mathematical. The beaming Wenger sisters, Edna and Grace, taught us Latin and English; Edna would always store her hanky in her cape.

The cafeteria was in the basement of the auditorium. We ate six to a table and couldn't be excused until everyone at the table had finished. So I should say we gobbled, not ate, to avoid being conspicuous. Would you want everybody else with their plates already emptied staring at you while you chewed and maybe dropped your noodles off your fork?

(They made the most wonderful scrambled eggs at that school. Once I asked one of the cafeteria cooks what else was in the eggs and she said cracker crumbs.)

Back in the dorm at night we did study some, I'm sure. But it was more fun sneaking around and conniving and discussing things. The elderly dean, we agreed, looked like a panda. We teased my roommate

about looking like a chipmunk. Another girl was an anteater (we never told *her* that), and somebody else a pig.

Away from school I was skipping the capes, some, and probably my hair was *sticking out*. Here, Donna Frey and Kendra Crist and Marcella Yoder and I (all of us dorm friends) must have been downtown, at one of those photo booths with just one stool and a green light that flashes and you have to quick run into the booth when it's your turn to be photographed, before the light comes back on. (For some reason I got to stay on the stool.) Do they still have these booths in department stores?

Some of my friends were already going out on dates. So I was pretty concerned about my own chances. The girl was supposed to sit in the middle of the front seat (or on the console, if the car had bucket seats). The boy was supposed to always open the door. The girl would sit in the car and wait for him to hop out and run around and open her door.

I was sixteen when Willie Longenecker broke my heart. He was older and hunky, with dreamy eyes. I guess he thought I looked good enough. We were having the first date (my very first date—we went somewhere to church in the evening). And he said we'd be going on the second date as planned, but then that was going to be it. I had to carry on, burdened with the knowledge. Willie Longenecker, you were rotten to me.

I wasn't managing to be especially popular. Fred Garber took me out, because Linda had broken up with him (to try to figure out if she was really serious about him), and he guessed taking me out a couple of times would cause her to be jealous and make up her mind. It was an effective approach but not a whole lot of fun for me, considering the situation.

I did get to be maid of honor at their wedding.

4. Flapping My Wings

Fred and Linda took pretty long getting actually married, so the wedding wasn't till after I'd gone off to the Mennonite college in Virginia. My boyfriend from Ohio brought me home for the wedding.

Dorm life wasn't so restricted at college. We couldn't be out all hours, but nobody was patrolling the halls. Here again, I studied some. I also sat on Nancy Horst's fig bars (she maybe still hasn't forgiven me) and played "Burdens Are Lifted at Calvary" on the piano for Mr. Martin's English class.

Sharon Hurst and I went down to the lounge one day in the basement of the girls' dorm, where there were sofas and an old piano and where female students left their coats and books while they ate lunch. (The cafeteria and a couple of classrooms were also in the

The ceremony wasn't outdoors; we just stood in front of those bushes for the pictures. I'm next to the bride. You can see that my covering has shrunk considerably.

dorm basement.) Sharon wasn't altogether dressed, but it was okay—we'd gone down an inside stairway. My roommate, Phyllis Pellman, was in Mr. Martin's classroom next door, on the other side of the lounge wall, and we were going to entertain Phyllis.

We proceeded to belt out "Burdens Are Lifted" in an outstanding hillbilly fashion while I pounded some chords on the piano. And suddenly Mr. Martin was standing right there in the doorway (he'd opened the door), and Sharon was cowering behind me in her maroon blouse and little black half slip, and Mr. Martin was grinning and asking would we like to come over and singing for the class. We assured him we wouldn't. He shut the door and we hurried back upstairs.

Besides sing hillbilly, Sharon could talk like a duck. She'd flatten her lips into a sort of duck shape. Once when Truman Brunk, the campus pastor, was walking by the dorm, Sharon quacked, "Truman, Truman, you're my love," out the window. But I don't suppose he ever knew what was going on.

The schoolgirls were growing up, although by now you must be wondering. We were trying our wings (feathers, whatever). And changing.

I'd come to college determined to prove to everybody back home, or to myself at least, that you didn't have to change when you went away. (College, it was believed, changed people; they came back different.) The Mennonites in Virginia weren't as plain as the ones in Pennsylvania. So I knew it would take some effort to be stalwart. Or not too compromised, anyway.

Here you've been thinking that with all the trialsomeness of growing up I was just biding my time, waiting till I could break loose and tap my pointy toes and throw all the rules in the trash can. Certainly I'd cried and argued with my parents. But the fact is, I believed there was some virtue in plainness, some truth in those rules. I wanted to be liked and admired, not be bad, necessarily. I didn't want to leave God, leave the church.

And I didn't leave. But I did change.

More and more Mennonites were changing, even the Mennonites back home, and the regulations got pushed aside and forgotten. As it turned out, there was still God who loved me, and a people with whom I belonged. (And it still mattered that we lived right and loved our enemies.)

But how, do you suppose, could we just forget about those rules? People like me who'd *believed* (however grudgingly)?

Did forgetting, for me, have something to do with the play, maybe?

I was Miss Mowbray in *The Bishop's Mantle.*

I'd always liked plays. One summertime back in Steelton I'd hung a bedspread over the clothesline on the porch (stage) and hauled chairs out to the yard (auditorium) and started gearing up for some sort of show. But instead I'd gotten a terrible bellyache and ended up in the hospital with appendicitis. So already then the theater held a certain danger.

In *The Bishop's Mantle*, put on at the college, Miss Mowbray was the rector's secretary, dull and somewhat dizzy. (I was a freshman and just glad to get a role, any role.) So of course I was supposed to look dull. But before the first dress rehearsal the makeup people did me wrong, and I came out with exotic hair and too much stuff on my face. I guess I looked ravishing, nearly; the people I passed by looked at me strangely. Hereafter an effort was made by the makeup department to uglify rather than beautify me. But the brief moment of glory, being looked at like that, was intoxicating. The taste was ever so sweet.

How could I any longer endure being *plain*?

The cast of The Bishop's Mantle; *Miss Mowbray is second from the left. (Look how the toes of my shoes are curled up, like Aladdin's.)*

To this very day, however, glory (even sweet glory) does not seem to me a proper justification for abandoning one's principles.

Flapping my wings ever so loudly, I eventually hacked my hair all the way short and wore blue jeans and awful skirts that hardly reached below my rear end. And no covering.

I am forever indebted to Mark Fly. Ruth Ann Ziegler lived next door to me in the college dorm my senior year, and Mark was her boyfriend; he could be talkative and friendly, and one day he told me my eyeliner was on too heavy. He was right, of course. Excess is an easy trap, and there are many ways to make oneself look odd. I don't wear makeup at all, anymore.

Maybe you're wondering what this old Steelton picture is for. It's just some snow, and my sister and little brothers, and the clothesline.

5.
Eleven Bowls of Tulips

The astonishing thing is this. All those Mennonite school girlfriends I've told you about, and none of us has to my knowledge turned miserable and ugly and neurotic. I think being plain when we were young must not have been completely devastating.

I almost wonder if it was good for us.

Maybe if you don't have any troubles at all, you don't ever quite grow up.

What sort of hardships were mine, anyway? Nobody was *out to get me*. The Mennonite bishops weren't making up rules to be mean; they wanted us kept safe from the world, and pure. Certainly *different* was better than *wrong*, if those were the only choices.

I know it was hard for my mother, having to watch me make my mistakes (what I considered victories).

Also having to wonder if she was doing something wrong herself, with things not turning out like they were supposed to. But I think hardly anything ever ends up quite the way we expect.

Last fall I was up at my parents' house in Pennsylvania helping my mother quilt. She was so happy I'd come; two of my sisters-in-law had come, too, and we sat lined up along the quilting frame, telling stories and shooing away the little children. My mother had sewed eleven bowls of tulips onto her quilt top, and now we were stitching fancy lines around the tulips and along the edges of the quilt. It was a comfort, quilting with my mother and being together.

A few weeks later we were up there again, for Sunday dinner. Just my family, this time—Paulson and me and our kids. My mother had made a wonderful cake for my birthday, with coconut and orange rinds in the icing. She had on a dark blue jacket and a shiny white blouse and a long, narrow skirt with a *kick pleat,* mind you. But she still wore her bun and covering. I guess I would be disappointed in her if she ever *didn't,* because she and my father have always maintained that there should be long hair and coverings. It could even be that they are right.

(That Sunday I shuffled through my parents' boxfuls of old photographs and carted some of them along home with me. I didn't want to tell my mother what for; what if she wouldn't let me take the pictures? So I hope she's not too disconcerted by all this.)

I saw Ginnie Mummau not long ago at her house (not the one where she grew up). She and her husband and all her children, plus her very old mother. Ginnie was wanting to take me around the farm in this funny Jeep-like vehicle they have with all the doors taken off. So I rode in the back and shivered and stared in wonderment at the huge fields of celery and broccoli and cauliflower.

Ginnie is the only one of us school friends who is still plain. She is even plainer than she was growing up. She wears a covering and black stockings and black shoes, and dresses with long sleeves and capes, like all the women do at her church. (The one she joined after she grew up, when so many of the other Mennonite churches were forgetting about the rules.)

Gentle, shining Ginnie, so lively and funny. And beautiful.

That day at her house we jabbered and laughed and finally hugged goodbye. I left all warmed in my heart and blessed.

It is to Ginnie I'll be sending this story. And to Mark Fly. And to my parents who have surely loved me.

About the Author

Shirley Kurtz has authored several children's books—*The Boy and the Quilt, Applesauce,* and *Birthday Chickens* (Good Books). She writes occasional articles for Mennonite Church periodicals.

She lives with her husband and children near Keyser, West Virginia. They attend a Mennonite congregation at Pinto, Maryland.